BIRDS
OF PREY

Design
David West
Children's Book Design
Illustrations
Louise Nevett
Tessa Barwick
Picture Research
Cecilia West-Baker
Consultant
Dr Philip J K Burton

© Aladdin Books Ltd

Designed and produced by
Aladdin Books Ltd
70 Old Compton Street
LONDON W1

First published in the
United States in 1987 by
Gloucester Press
387 Park Avenue South
New York NY 10016

ISBN 0-531-17050-0
Library of Congress Catalog
Card Number 87-80467

Printed in Belgium

This book tells you about birds of prey – how they live, how to recognize them and how they survive in today's changing world. Find out some surprising facts in the boxes on each page. The Spotters' Guide at the back will help you identify different birds when you see them.

 **or**

The little square shows you the size of the bird. Each side represents about 3 feet (1m).

A red square means that a bird is in need of protection. Turn to the Survival File.

The picture opposite is of a Snowy Owl from the Arctic Circle

FIRST SIGHT

BIRDS OF PREY

Kate Petty

GLOUCESTER PRESS

New York · London · Toronto · Sydney

Introduction

Eagles, hawks, falcons, vultures, owls – these are all birds of prey, or "raptors" as they are sometimes called. Most of them are large birds with hooked beaks and long, sharp talons. They need these to hunt and kill other birds and animals for their food.

Like many wild animals today, birds of prey are endangered because of changes in the environment. The forests they live in are cut down, or the rivers they fish from are polluted. Thirty years ago some birds of prey nearly became extinct. Many were shot and trapped. Others were poisoned by pesticides. Now many people are doing what they can to protect them and make sure that they are still around for you and your own children to see.

◁ **Bald Eagle, no longer a common bird of prey**

Birds you might see

A Buzzard soaring above the fields is quite a common sight in Europe. So is its cousin, the Red-tailed Hawk, in the United States.

If you see any large bird soaring, hovering or swooping, it could be a bird of prey. It might be a Kestrel hovering in the air near a highway. Or you might spot a Sparrowhawk skimming the treetops, making all the smaller birds call out in alarm.

Birdwatchers learn to recognize birds of prey from a distance by the shape of their wings and tail feathers. You will need a pair of binoculars to get a good look at their colors and markings. Then you can use the Spotters' Guide to help you identify the birds.

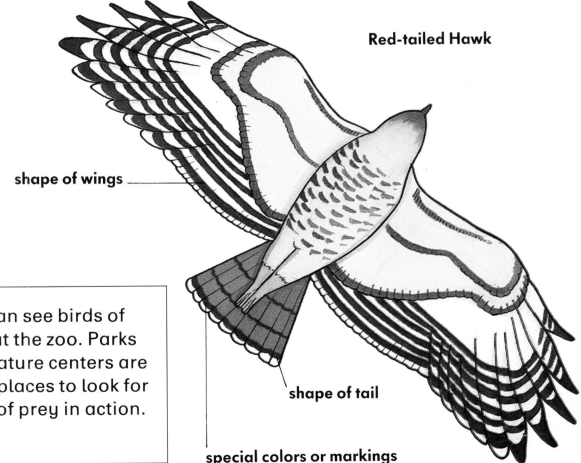

Red-tailed Hawk

shape of wings

shape of tail

special colors or markings

You can see birds of prey at the zoo. Parks and nature centers are good places to look for birds of prey in action.

7

◁ **Common Buzzard with its kill**

Keen sight

All hunting birds need excellent eyesight for spotting their prey from a long way off. Some of them use a favorite rock or perch as a lookout point. A Kestrel hovers in the air when it is searching for food. It scans the field below with a steady gaze and then swoops down on its victim. It can see a grasshopper in the grass from 300 feet (100m) away.

Birds of prey have big eyes which are often brightly colored. The Black-shouldered Kite has beautiful coral-red eyes. They are protected from the sun by feathery "eyebrows."

Both these birds are looking at you! Birds of prey look separately out of each eye to see sideways but they use both eyes together to see straight ahead.

Black-shouldered Kite

A Kestrel is quite likely to use a nest box if you make one. Kestrels usually lay their eggs in rocky hollows or in another bird's old nest.

◁ **Kestrel hovering**

Talons that kill

Most birds of prey use their feet to grab and kill their victims. Each foot has four toes with long, curved claws called talons. The three forward-pointing toes are for grasping. The talon on the back toe is like a knife which stabs the prey.

The long middle toe of the Sparrowhawk helps it to snatch little birds in mid-air. The Osprey lives on fish. Its feet are specially adapted for fishing, with two toes pointing forward and two pointing backward. The undersides of the toes are covered in tiny sharp spikes, called spicules, for gripping slithery fish. The powerful grasp of the Harpy Eagle's claws can crush a monkey or a sloth in a very few seconds.

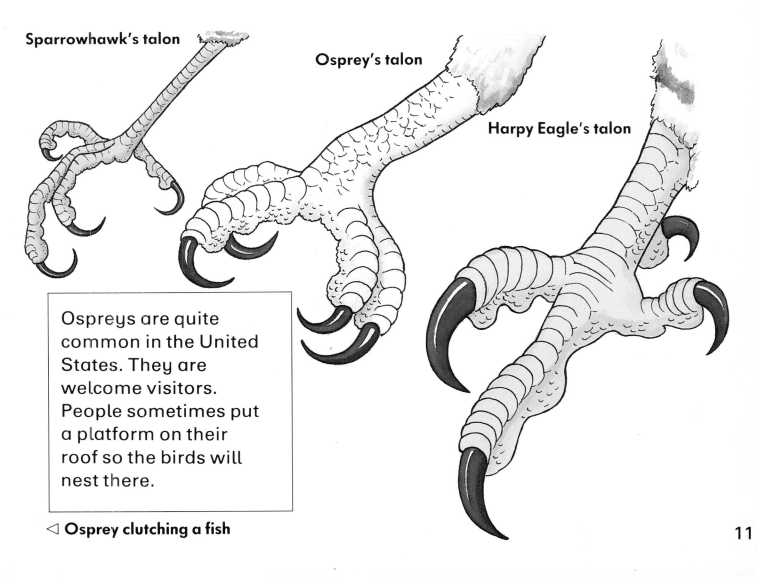

Sparrowhawk's talon

Osprey's talon

Harpy Eagle's talon

Ospreys are quite common in the United States. They are welcome visitors. People sometimes put a platform on their roof so the birds will nest there.

◁ **Osprey clutching a fish**

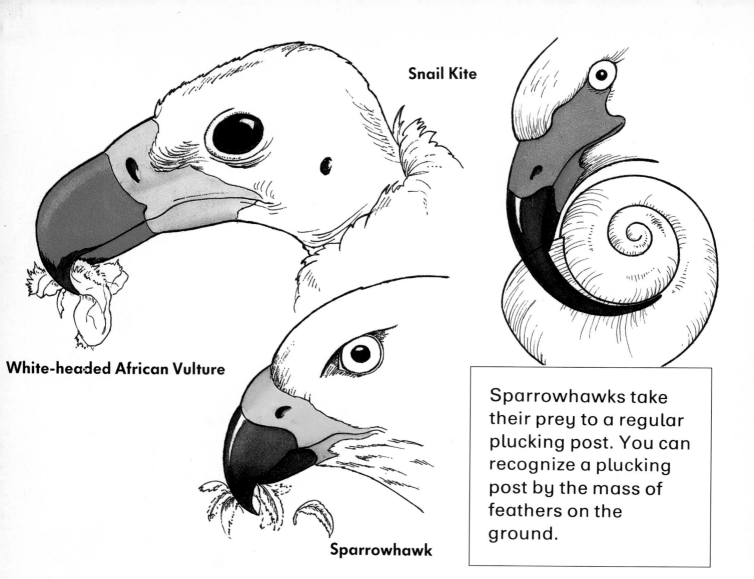

Snail Kite

White-headed African Vulture

Sparrowhawk

Sparrowhawks take their prey to a regular plucking post. You can recognize a plucking post by the mass of feathers on the ground.

Beaks for feeding

All raptors have sharp, hooked beaks for tearing up prey after they have killed it with their talons. Parent birds will shred the meat into tiny pieces to feed their young.

Hawks which kill other birds, like the fierce little Sparrowhawk and the Sharp-shinned Hawk, use their beaks to pluck the feathers from their prey. Eagles and vultures need to rip the flesh off large carcasses, so their beaks are very powerful. The Snail Kite's beak is exactly the right shape for extracting snails from their shells.

Sparrowhawk plucking its prey ▷

On the wing

The shape of a bird's wings tells you something about the way it flies. Eagles and vultures have long wings to soar on currents of warm air called thermals. Like many falcons, Kestrels have pointed wings for fast flying. They can beat their wings rapidly to hover as well. Woodland birds of prey like the Forest Falcon have more rounded wings for flying among trees.

In the spring some birds put on a wonderful show of aerobatics. When Montagu's Harrier is showing off to his mate he swoops and somersaults, climbs and dives again. Then the female joins in, rolling over as she flies to take a piece of food offered by her mate. Harriers are long-distance fliers, sometimes covering 150 miles (250km) a day on their way to warmer countries.

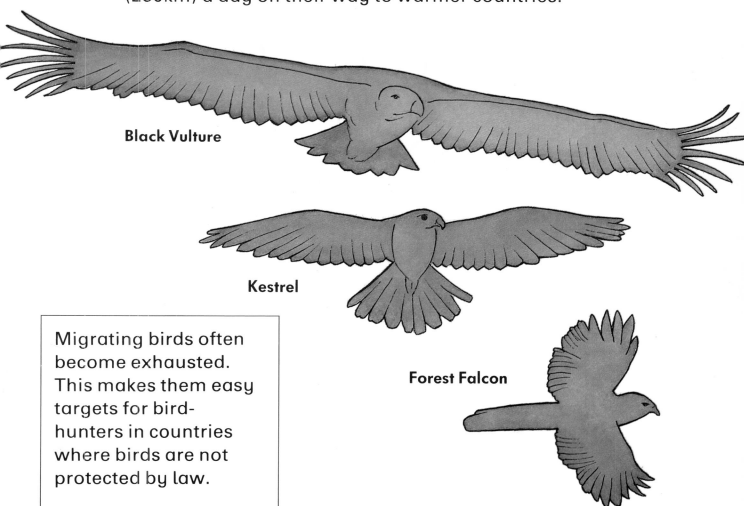

Black Vulture

Kestrel

Forest Falcon

Migrating birds often become exhausted. This makes them easy targets for bird-hunters in countries where birds are not protected by law.

◁ **Montagu's Harrier, a long-distance flier**

15

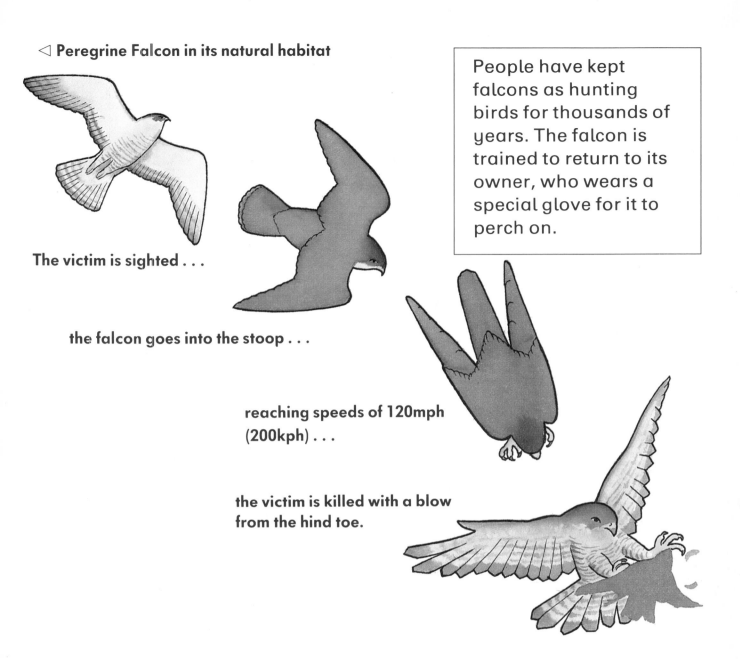

◁ **Peregrine Falcon in its natural habitat**

The victim is sighted . . .

the falcon goes into the stoop . . .

reaching speeds of 120mph (200kph) . . .

the victim is killed with a blow from the hind toe.

People have kept falcons as hunting birds for thousands of years. The falcon is trained to return to its owner, who wears a special glove for it to perch on.

The streamlined hunter

The Peregrine Falcon's spectacular steep dive for its prey is called a "stoop." Once common all over the world, the Peregrine Falcon almost completely disappeared in some places about thirty years ago. The Peregrine feeds off smaller birds. These little birds were eating grain which had been sprayed with pesticide. The poison built up inside the falcons. It stopped their eggs forming properly, so the Peregrines almost died out. People are more careful with poisonous pesticides now, and Peregrines are slowly becoming more common again.

The silent hunters

Most owls hunt at night so they need to see in the dark. They also have excellent hearing and special soft feathers for silent flight.

There are 140 different sorts of owls in the world. Small owls, like the Little Owl, are no bigger than 8 inches (20cm). The biggest, the Eagle Owl, is about 28 inches (70cm) long.

Barn Owls were once found on farms all over Europe and America. They were useful to farmers because they killed rats. Now many of their homes, particularly in old barns and elm trees, have been destroyed.

Birds of prey can't easily digest bones and feathers, so they bring these up again in a tight little ball called a pellet. You can often tell what an owl has eaten by examining one of its pellets.

owl pellets

Large owls eat all these creatures. They will sometimes swallow them whole.

rabbits

frogs

mice

moles

grasshoppers

field voles

Barn Owl hunting in the snow ▷

Nesting

This Golden Eagle and her mate come back to the same nest year after year. Their nest is called an eyrie. It is made of twigs and lined with leaves. They build it high up where no harm can come to the eggs. The eagle is a fierce hunter but a gentle mother. She sits on the eggs for six weeks before they hatch. The chicks learn to fly when they are twelve weeks old but both parents still feed them for many weeks after that.

Some birds which fly and hunt low down build their nests on the ground. Marsh Harriers make their nests in the reeds. The male feeds the female when she is sitting on the eggs. She flies off the nest and rolls over in the air to take the food from him.

◁ **Marsh Harrier with its young**

The eggs of most birds of prey are white speckled with brown. NEVER, EVER steal eggs from a nest or disturb nesting birds. You could be breaking the law.

◁ **Golden Eagle with its young**

The majestic eagles

Eagles are the largest and most powerful birds of prey.
Compare them with others in the Spotters' Guide.
Many of them are over 28 inches (70cm) long with a
wingspan of over 6 feet (2m). The Harpy Eagle from the
South American jungle is the largest of all. The biggest
one recorded weighed over 25 pounds (12kg). It preys
on monkeys, oppossums and macaws.

People all over the world have used the eagle as a
symbol of strength and power. The Bald Eagle is the
national emblem of the United States, though today it
is a fairly rare bird found mostly in Alaska.

Eagles can kill animals
that are much bigger
than themselves. They
are sometimes
responsible for killing
sheep. More often they
prey on smaller
creatures that they can
carry off.

**The flag of the President of the
United States shows a Bald Eagle**

Rare Harpy Eagle from the South American jungle ▷

Nature's cleaners

Vultures do not usually kill for their food. They feed off "carrion" — the flesh of dead animals. Most vultures live in hot, wild places. The White-backed Vulture lives in Asia. The King Vulture is quite common in Central and Southern America. They soar on the rising hot air and fly high, searching for dead or dying animals. They do a useful job eating carrion which would otherwise rot in the hot sun. Their heads and necks are bald so they can thrust them deep into the carcasses.

Condors are vultures. The Andean Condor is the largest of all vultures. The California Condor from North America is sadly now almost extinct.

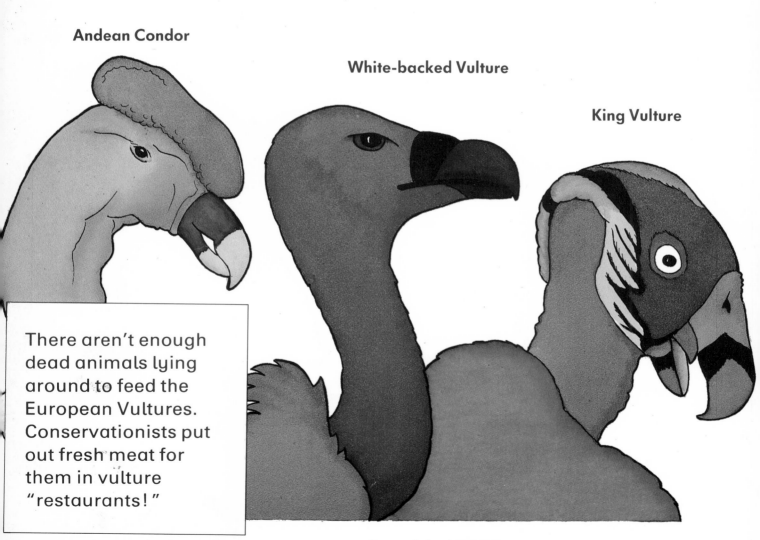

Andean Condor

White-backed Vulture

King Vulture

There aren't enough dead animals lying around to feed the European Vultures. Conservationists put out fresh meat for them in vulture "restaurants!"

One of the few remaining California Condors ▷

Unusual birds of prey

The Secretary Bird lives in the African grasslands. It runs on its long legs more often than it flies. As well as insects and small mammals the Secretary Bird eats tortoises and snakes. It kicks them to death with its large feet. This one has caught a frog. It is called a Secretary Bird after the secretaries of 200 years ago, when men wore wigs. Secretaries stuck their quill pens in their wigs for safekeeping!

The African Harrier Hawk has legs which bend both ways. It searches all around a hole in a tree trunk with its foot. It can grab a bat from the top of the hole or a baby bird from the bottom.

African Harrier Hawk

Secretary Birds are sometimes kept in captivity in South Africa to keep down snakes and rats.

◁ **Secretary Bird demolishing a frog**

27

Survival file

Many birds of prey must struggle to survive in our changing world. Like all animals, they suffer when their habitat is destroyed or altered. Many farmers and gamekeepers think they are pests and try to get rid of them. More and more people use cars, which bring hikers and photographers tramping closer than ever to their hidden homes.

Young male Sparrowhawk caught in a pole trap

So many Ospreys were killed in Britain that there were none left. Now a few pairs have arrived from Scandinavia. Their closely guarded nests are kept secret so they can breed in peace.

The Snail Kite eats one thing — apple snails. Changes in the countryside made the snail scarce, so feeding refuges have been built for the birds in places where there are still plenty of snails for them.

Male Snail Kite

You now need a license to keep a Peregrine Falcon in Britain. Twenty years ago in eastern America the Peregrine Falcon disappeared altogether. Now they are being bred in captivity.

Barn Owls lose their hunting grounds and nesting sites when trees are cut down and old farm buildings are modernized. Nest boxes built near their old nesting sites are bringing some of them back.

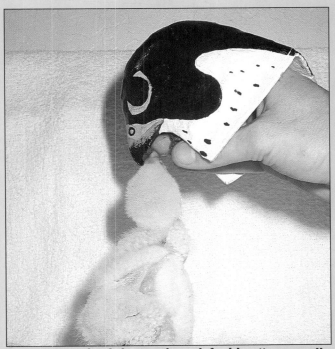

Peregrine chick being hand-fed by "parent"

Montagu's Harrier likes to nest in cornfields. Farmers can help conservationists to protect the birds by not spraying their nesting sites and by waiting for the chicks to grow before cutting the crops.

Golden Eagles were persecuted by farmers and gamekeepers and egg collectors robbed their nests. Now it is illegal to harm a Golden Eagle or go near its nest.

There are only three California Condors left in the wild. Conservationists have made refuges for them and feed them fresh meat. Now they are trying to rear chicks in captivity.

Spotters' guide

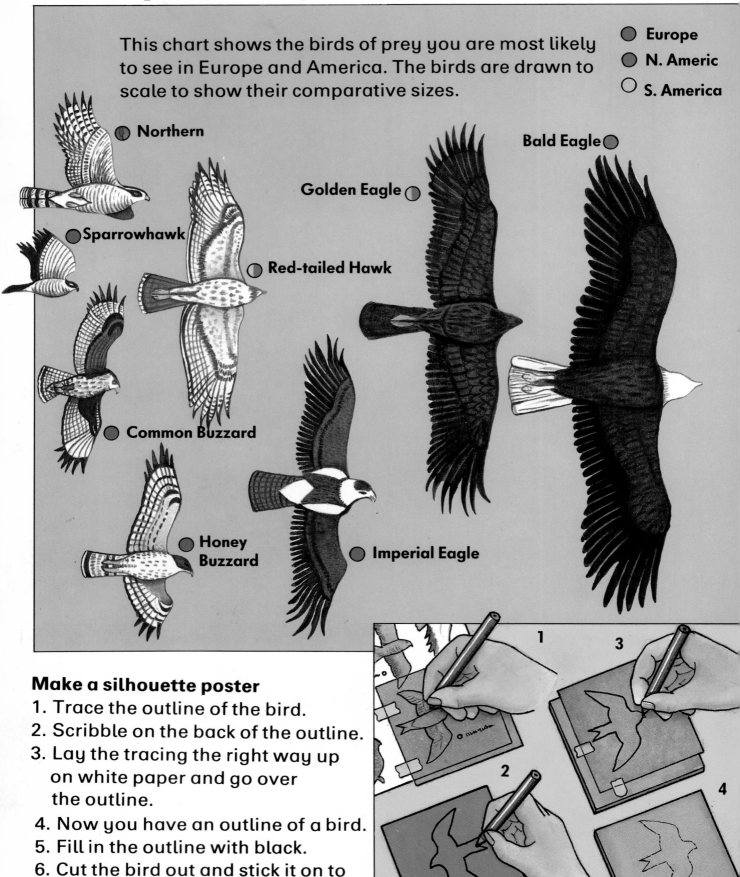

This chart shows the birds of prey you are most likely to see in Europe and America. The birds are drawn to scale to show their comparative sizes.

- Europe
- N. Americ
- S. America

Northern

Sparrowhawk

Golden Eagle

Bald Eagle

Red-tailed Hawk

Common Buzzard

Honey Buzzard

Imperial Eagle

Make a silhouette poster
1. Trace the outline of the bird.
2. Scribble on the back of the outline.
3. Lay the tracing the right way up on white paper and go over the outline.
4. Now you have an outline of a bird.
5. Fill in the outline with black.
6. Cut the bird out and stick it on to your poster.

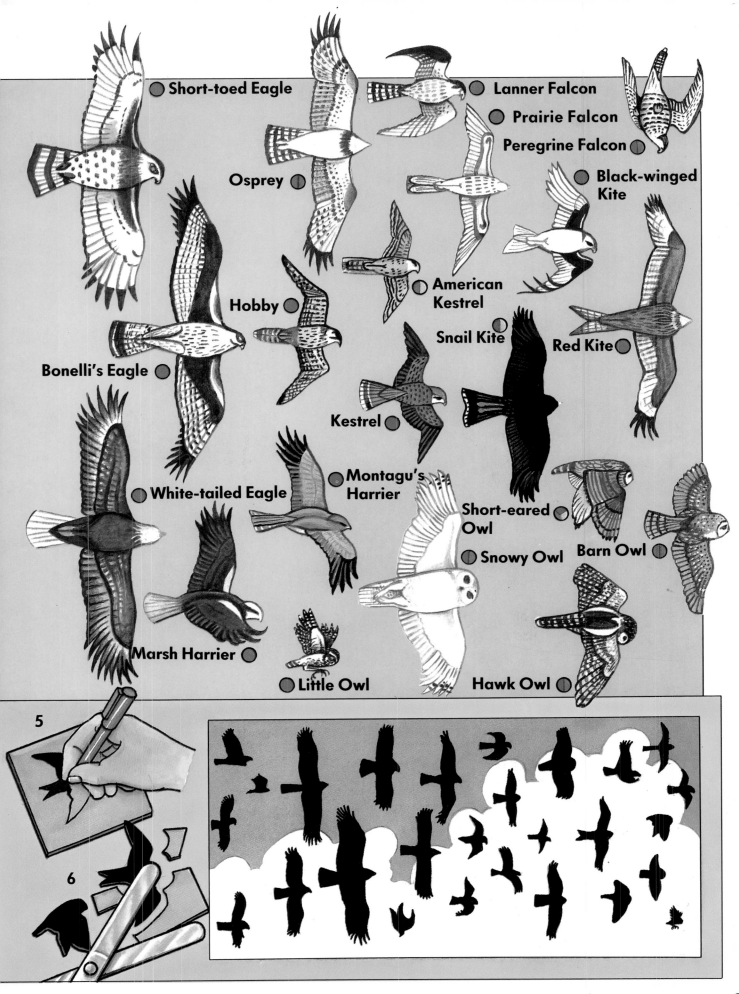

Short-toed Eagle

Lanner Falcon

Prairie Falcon

Peregrine Falcon

Osprey

Black-winged Kite

American Kestrel

Hobby

Snail Kite

Red Kite

Bonelli's Eagle

Kestrel

White-tailed Eagle

Montagu's Harrier

Short-eared Owl

Snowy Owl

Barn Owl

Marsh Harrier

Little Owl

Hawk Owl

5

6

Index

The picture on the cover shows the tiny North American Saw-Whet Owl

Photographic credits
Cover and page 20: Zefa; title page and pages 4, 10, 13, 21, 23, 26 and 29: Bruce Coleman; page 6: John Hawkins/Eric and David Hoskings; pages 8, 14 and 19: Ardea; page 16: Eric and David Hoskings; page 28: Andrew Cleave/Nature Photographers; page 29: Kevin Carlson/Nature Photographers.

PRINTED IN BELGIUM BY proost INTERNATIONAL BOOK PRODUCTION